Secrets that Sparkle
(and Secrets that Sting)

Written by Joy Stephenson-Laws

For Kyle, Erica and every child finding their voice—
May you always know it's brave to be heard.

Secrets That Sparkle (and Secrets That Sting)

A Rhyming Picture Book for Ages 5+

Illustrations by Nzephany Madrigal Uzoka
Edited by Tim Scerba
Printed in the United States of America

Some secrets are sweet,
like a gift in a box,

But some hide a feeling
that squiggles and knocks.

Let's learn which to keep, and
which we should share—

Because safe kids are strong,
and grown-ups will care!

2

Some secrets are giggles just
waiting to pop,

Like bubbles that bounce and
never quite stop!

Like hiding a card for your
dad's birthday cheer,

Then shouting
"SURPRISE!"
when he finally comes near.

4

Or sneak a tall cupcake,
frosting piled high,
Then tiptoe to snack when
no grown-ups walk by.

These secrets are short and
they sparkle with cheer—
And soon everyone's laughing
from ear to ear!

But some other secrets feel
squiggly and wrong,

Like a sock in your shoe that's
been there too long.

They sit in your belly like
stones in a pile,

And don't come with cupcakes,
or giggles, or smiles.

If someone you trust— like cousin or friend—

Whispers, "Keep this secret— no grown-ups must know."

Says, "Tell no one else—
just hold it inside,"

That's not birthday fun—that's
not how play should go.

10

That's not a surprise with
balloons in the air—

That's a secret that isn't
happy or fair.

If your tummy
feels twisty
and something
feels yuck,

That's not a
secret—you
don't have to
get stuck!

You can tell Mom, or your
teacher at school,

A coach or grandma—safe
grown-ups are cool!

They'll listen with care—
they'll always be there,

They'll give you big hugs and
show that they care.

You won't be in trouble.
You're never to blame.
You're not bad.
You're not wrong.
You're not part of the shame.

Telling is brave,
and it opens the door—

To hugs, to comfort, and
joy at your core.

16

If someone you know tries
to make you feel small,

Or tells you, "Be quiet.
Don't tell that at all."
17

That's not a secret to carry or keep—
that's one to let out, not bury down deep.

Even someone you once held dear—
an uncle, coach, or neighbor near,

If words or touch feel
wrong or unclear,

Tell a safe grown—up—
your voice will be heard.
20

You don't have to
hide, you don't
have to lie—

You don't have to
swallow your
feelings and cry.

21

You can whisper it softly,
or draw it in crayon,

You can shout it out
loudly—like a brave,
roaring lion!

Grown-ups who love you
will listen with care,

They'll believe what you say,
and they'll always be there.

You're not in trouble, and
you didn't do wrong,

You're telling the truth,
and that makes you strong.

So let's remember
this secret for sure—

That your body is yours,
from your toes to your core.

No one gets to touch or
ask things unkind,
And secrets that hurt?
You can always unwind.

Some secrets are silly—
like a birthday surprise,
Or hiding a snack right
under Dad's eyes!

27

But secrets that scare you or make you feel bad,

Aren't secrets to keep—they're ones to be had.

By someone who listens, who loves, and who knows,

That your truth is your power, wherever it goes!

28

So if there's a secret that
weighs like a rock,

Don't wait—go ahead.
It's okay to talk.

Telling the truth is the
bravest thing yet,

And it helps your heart
feel safe, not upset.

30

You are kind.
You are strong.
You are smart
as can be.

Your voice is your magic.

Your truth sets you free.

Dear Grown-Ups,

Children hold many secrets—some
sparkle with joy, others weigh heavy with
worry.

This book shows which to keep close and
which to share bravely.

Telling a troubling secret is both
safe—and never their fault.

Please offer a calm, caring space where
your child can share anything that feels
too big to carry alone.

Joy Stephenson-Laws

About the Author

Joy Stephenson-Laws, Esq., is a dynamic and deeply committed holistic health coach whose life's work centers around empowering individuals—physically, mentally, emotionally, and spiritually. As the founder and president of Proactive Health Labs (pH Labs) and the managing partner of Stephenson, Acquisto & Colman, one of the nation's leading healthcare litigation firms, Joy brings over 40 years of expertise in healthcare advocacy, wellness education, and legal leadership.

With a foundational commitment to physical health, Joy has expanded her vision to embrace the vibrant synergy of mind, body, and spirit, understanding that true well-being encompasses the whole person. Trained through the Foundation for Holistic Life Coaching, Joy combines scientific insight, emotional intelligence, and heart-centered support to empower families to nurture resilient, confident, and emotionally balanced children.

Joy's passion is rooted in preventing needless suffering by promoting education, proactive health choices, and early intervention. Her holistic coaching guides children and families toward clarity, confidence, and empowered decision-making, ensuring they feel supported in every aspect of their well-being.

She is the author of Minerals — The Forgotten Nutrient: Your Secret Weapon for Getting and Staying Healthy and regularly contributes to media outlets. Joy is currently developing poetry aimed at inspiring emotional health and personal growth for readers of all ages.

To learn more about Joy and her holistic approach to health, visit https://phlabs.org/coaches-counselors/joy-stephenson-laws

Secrets That Sparkle (and Secrets That Sting) is a rhyming, read-aloud picture book that gently empowers young children to tell the difference between "fun secrets" (like surprise parties and hidden cupcakes) and unsafe ones that make them feel scared, confused, or uncomfortable. With playful language, clear contrasts, and emotionally safe storytelling, this book teaches children how to recognize secrets that should never be kept—and how to speak up with courage.

Written with 5-year-olds in mind, this book supports conversations around body autonomy, unsafe touch, and emotional trust. Ideal for parents, educators, therapists, and school counselors, it has a fully lyrical narrative and emotionally uplifting tone.